SIMPLICITY of WORSHIP

E. L. WARREN

Simplicity of Worship
by E.L. Warren

Copyright © 2018 by E.L. Warren

Published by Dream Releaser Publishing

Print ISBN: 978-1-943294-86-2

Simplicity of Worship is also available on Amazon Kindle, Barnes & Noble Nook and Apple iBooks.

Contents

Foreword

AS SOON AS I BEGAN TO READ the manuscript for this book by my longtime friend and mentor, Bishop E.L. Warren, I was immediately drawn back to the time we first met. When you know the integrity, personality, and the passion of the person you write about, it's important to note how special our relationships are. I recalled the powerful women's conferences that I was invited to minister in praise and worship in Quincy, IL. Being a male, at first, I wondered, "Why me?" I'm so glad I listened to the wisdom of my late wife Shirley and the Holy Spirit and accepted the invitation. I had the opportunity to make many new friends at these events, and I was personally impacted by them. I still remember the words spoken over me by Bishop and the speakers that have gone on to new heights in ministry and influence.

Also, who can ever forget the warm hospitality displayed by Bishop's lovely wife, who we refer to as Lady Ella! The times we gathered around the dinner table in the Warren home produced lasting memories and deep, deep friendships. And who doesn't love a good meal?

As I was reading this power-packed book, it was like having a personal conversation with the author. I believe that's one of the secrets to a well-written document that will impact the lives of others for many generations.

As a perpetual learner, I received something fresh and new—and began to underline my favorite quotes.

God is seeking those who will worship Him in spirit and truth.

Now I have an even deeper understanding as to what happened in the summer of 2012 when the doctor said, "Mr. Chapman, I wish I had better news, but you have prostate cancer that has spread to your bones." The pain in my right shoulder was so severe I could not drive my car, play the piano, or dress. Praise God, there is no pain as I type this. I will never forget the day I was sitting in my favorite chair and was caught away into worship. The next thing I knew, my arms were lifted high in His presence and my mobility was restored completely. It may sound trivial, but I worship when I'm doing laundry and other household chores.

That's how grateful I am to be able to do the things we take for granted every day. One of my deepest concerns, this is a personal observation: In this high-tech age, we are creating more watchers than worshipers. I'm not against arts in the church but when the attention is on performance rather than His presence, it becomes entertainment more than worship.

I absolutely love this book, and it's my prayer that it will cause us to go back and refocus on the real meaning and importance of worship. God is seeking those who will worship Him in spirit and truth.

Thank you, Bishop Warren, for writing a timely book that can be used as a study guide and a powerful teaching tool for many generations to come.

Morris Chapman
Songwriter, Worship Leader, Minister

Endorsements

I recommend *Simplicity of Worship* by Dr. E.L. Warren to anyone seeking higher heights and deeper depths in Christ! *Simplicity of Worship* is riveting, it simplified something that seemed to be a complicated mystery: worship. As a worship leader, I have been seeking this instruction since the onset of my worship ministry. Upon completing this book, immediately my entire ministry was shifted and catapulted to the next level. I am forever changed and all the more encouraged. Thank you, Bishop Warren, for sharing this "treasure" of the secret place!

James M. Ferguson, II
Minister of Music
Abundant Faith Church of Integrity
Milwaukee, WI

Simplicity of Worship is in no way simplistic. It is a mature evaluation of the heart of God and His desire for us to be an intimate part of His life. This book opens the blinded mind, destroys the perverted concept of praise and sets us on a path of honesty, righteousness, and love!

Dr. Warren takes us on a journey of truth, self-evaluation, and discovery that leads us into God's heart, into His presence and back to our world with His will and desire stamped on our heart! Thank you, Dr. Warren, for forging a path of light that will enable us to worship God in Spirit and truth.

Charlotte Dotts
Pastor
Word of Life Ministries
Bloomington, IL

Bishop E.L. Warren has released this truth for such a time as this! Simplicity means: not complicated, not difficult to understand. We have witnessed and do witness, on a daily and weekly basis, the presentation of worship reduced to half-hearted verbal expressions, talented song singing, and masterful musicians. With all of that, where was God? Did those elements create the atmosphere for our Lord to inhabit, to dwell in, to remain? The answer is no. Therefore, without the presence of the Lord through the worship, we experience the lack of manifestations in our lives, homes, and communities.

This book will, without doubt, transform nations and generations, present and to come. *Simplicity of Worship* walks us through the understanding of "true worship" which the Father is seeking (John 4:23) versus what is presumed as worship. In our desire to be like Jesus, we discover that there are simple missing pieces that Jesus Himself did daily that we must also do.

Engage and enjoy this Divine writing. It is definitely refreshing and yet enlightening. I personally appreciate the content and structure of the book. The intent to impact every reader is realized with the accountability factor.

Allow *Simplicity of Worship* to strengthen your personal relationship with Jesus Christ, as well as activate manifestations in every area of your life. Thank you, Bishop Warren, for this powerful life-changing tool of truth.

Elder Shadonn Becton-Ross
Worship Leader
Pursuit of God Church
Memphis, TN

I was excited to hear about Dr. Warren releasing a book on worship. He has been my pastor for over 38 years and I've always admired his ability, through the Holy Spirit, to shift the atmosphere—all because he is a true worshiper. In reading this book, it has catapulted me to a different place of daily commitment, setting my mind, and having a more heartfelt, confident, verbalized, expression of the greatness of God. I am seeking His attention without ceasing. This book has challenged my worship to the "next level."

Elder Resha Brock
Worship Leader
Cathedral of Worship
Quincy, IL

Simplicity of Worship is purely magnificent. The information Bishop Warren placed in this book is the necessary tool to change your perception of being intentional with your worship. Each chapter caused me to evaluate what I have been giving God in the area of worship and step by step what I'm required to give in order to increase the world framed around me. This book gave me a practical and spiritual transformation on how to give God clear praise and true worship. For those of you that are looking for your next encounter with God the Father, Jesus, and the Holy Spirit, this book is a must-read. Thank you, Bishop Warren, for sharing what the Lord has given you in this season.

Janie Boston
In the Dance Cafe

Introduction

I AM WRITING THIS BOOK to inspire you to enter into worship: to make it relevant, relative, and comprehensible—to encourage you to adopt worship as a lifestyle and enable you to convey it to others. This is what I have extracted and proven to be true worship from the Word of God that really works: how to carry it out, how to inspire others, and how to enter in so that you can touch God.

Many are talented, but when it comes to the reality of leading worship, there are times when something is lost in the transaction. You have people that are great singers but they can't lead you into worship and others who are great worshipers but can't sing at all. God has blessed me to be able to sing and worship. Allow me to convey the principles, ideas, and details that God has revealed to me about worship.

CHAPTER ONE

Simplicity of Worship

FIRST, LET'S LOOK AT JOHN 4:23 as a basic foundation for worship:

"But the hour cometh, and now is, when the true worshipers shall worship the Father in spirit and truth: for the Father seeketh such to worship him."

There has to be something off. There must be a problem when we sing all day and never get into the presence of God. Something is missing when we say all the right things, but it garners no response from Heaven. We can speak all the right words and sing all the right songs, but we're talking to a God that is seemingly not responding.

We sing so many songs—we call it praise and worship. We sing for so long and yet we don't pierce the heavens or actually go into His presence. This makes it difficult for ministry and for the teaching of the Word. Without His presence, we seem to be plowing against the grain; plowing stony ground. When this is the case, it takes longer for the message to be understood and for us to experience the freedom and the fluency of the Word in people's lives. It can be traced back to the worship *not doing its part*.

We lift our hands, we say the right words, we sing the right songs and yet we don't pierce Heaven.

We're going to look analytically at what's occurring. We're going to zero in on what is hindering us and why we don't seem to achieve an audience with Him. We lift our hands, we say the right words, we sing the right songs and yet we don't pierce Heaven. We preach the right things—but few are set free. What's hindering us? What do we need to do to turn this around?

Jesus is the reason why we must adopt the idea of worship. He was the worshiper of worshipers. He would say things like, "I don't do anything except what I see my Father do." Jesus had complete comprehension of *who* the Father was—He was 100% man and 100% God. So, everything that He did on the Earth, He did as a man full of God, not a god. He is our model. Therefore, we must begin to adopt what Jesus did.

"But the hour cometh, and now is, when the true worshipers shall worship the Father in spirit and truth: for the Father seeketh such to worship him" (John 4:23).

The word "worship" is used in this passage three times. First, "...the hour cometh, and now is, when the true worshipers..." In my Bible, the words of Jesus are printed in red. The words "true worshipers" are red—Jesus said that there are *true worshipers*. So, there's some who label themselves "worshipers" that are not. What is the Father looking for in a true worshiper?

What is the difference between what we're doing or saying and what He is seeking?

If Jesus says there are true worshipers, that would imply there are some with the title of "worshiper" that don't meet the qualifications. There are some who are going through the motions, but there's something missing. Why would Jesus say the true worshipers shall worship the Father in spirit and in truth? It seems that He's defining true worship as founded in truth and conveyed by the spirit. He is saying this what the Father is actually looking for.

Looking again at verse 23, "But the hour cometh, and now is, when... the Father seeketh such to worship Him." This verse says that all worship does not attract the Father's attention, which is why it says the *true* worshiper. The worship that is in spirit and truth is what the Father seeks; He seeks this type or He seeks such a worshiper.

The Father is looking for something that apparently we don't always convey. What is the difference between what we're doing or saying and what He is seeking? We say all the correct words, but it seems like we don't get the right response. What is the Father wanting us to do?

> "And it came to pass in those days, that He went out into a mountain to pray, and continued all night in prayer to God" (Luke 6:12).

The word "prayer" in this verse is translated "worship." The words "prayer" and "worship" are interchangeable. For the sake of clarity, the word "pray" in this Scripture, in the Greek, is the word that implies the act or expression of worship. In Luke 6:12, we could say, "It came to pass in those days, that He went out into a mountain to do the act of *worship* and He continued all night, *expressing His worship* to God." This is the Greek word *proseuchomai.*

If we don't believe or we don't have a working testimony of what we're saying, we are trying to flatter Him.

The definition of *proseuchomai* is the act of worship. Jesus incorporated worship as a part of His lifestyle. He went out and worshipped all night long, extending His verbal accolades upon the Father. He was displaying His appreciation to the Father, in the act of worship. Every time the word "worship" is found in the Scriptures, it's followed by "and said." Worship is spoken! When we worship, we *express* our worship. It cannot be done if we're mute. It has to be done with some accolades; proclamations about the One we are worshipping. There must be statements of how great He is; how grand He is.

If we're worshipping and it's not from our heart, it's just words.

God knows if we mean it or not. If we're worshipping and it's not from our heart, it's just words. Sometimes we say, "Isn't He wonderful," but it's just flattery. If we don't believe or we don't have a working testimony of what we're saying, we are trying to flatter Him. We are using words that don't really express the honesty of our hearts. You can't flatter God because He can see the heart. I've seen people say, "Let's give Him praise," and I can tell from the way they're clapping their hands that they really don't mean it. I tell people all the time, "Don't just patty cake God." If He's a great God, then there ought to be great praise that comes from our lives. You can't say, "What a great God," if you haven't been in a place where you've experienced His greatness—it comes off as mere jargon. Your words are going to have to be more than just flattery. They must be a declaration of His greatness; an expression of your knowledge of who He is.

In Luke 6:12 and Luke 18:1, it says "pray" in the King James, but it can be interchanged with the word "worship"—*proseuchomai*. We could say, "In those days He went out into the mountain to *worship* and continued all night, in the expression, and in the *act of worship*."

Praise deals with the acts of God, and worship deals with His person. When we seek to know the difference between praise and worship, we find that praise is talking about what *He has done* and worship speaks of *who He is*. If we are going to worship Him, we must have some experience or knowledge of who He is. We have to have encountered Him at some point, so that when we say, "He can do it," it's coming from a knowledge of who He is. It's tough to believe God can do something when we're not sure who He is! When we are sure of who He is, it's easy for us to convey what He's capable of doing, because His person backs up who He is.

If we are going to worship Him, we must have some experience or knowledge of who He is.

I don't think anything about saying, "We're going to shut the winter storm off, we're not going to allow it to come into this region." Why? Because I know that God owns the elements and that He is the Lord God of the elements. When I speak by the Holy Ghost, the elements recognize Him in my voice. Hallelujah! I know that it is God that is backing up what I'm saying, and I know full well that He can shut the elements down! The act or the expression of worship is what Jesus did all night.

> "And he spake a parable unto them to this end, that men ought always to pray, and not to faint" (Luke 18:1).

Again, we can interchange this word "pray" with the word "worship"—*proseuchomai*. We could read, "And He spake a parable to them to this end, that men ought *always to worship and if they do, they won't faint.*" Prayer and worship are one and the same. If our worship is an expression of God's greatness, then our prayer is likewise a verbalization of His greatness!

If our worship is an expression of God's greatness, then our prayer is likewise a verbalization of His greatness!

Isn't it tragic when we say we're praying and all we're doing is begging, wishing, and whining, instead of declaring and decreeing? Our prayer should be: "Father, I decree and declare that You are strong and You are powerful!"

I prayed for a lady going into surgery. I said, "Thank you God that You're already in the surgical suite. I thank you, God, that You're already there. Why? Because You're omnipresent. You're a God of precision, therefore the cut will be precise. I thank you, Father, that You will guide the surgeon's hand, there will be no slip up. There will be no incident, there will be no accident. Why? Because You are God, sovereign and supreme!"

That's the kind of prayer or worship God is wanting, rather than, "If it be Your will Lord, keep her during the surgery; let no hurt, harm, or danger come, You're able."

We need to pray from a stronger level of faith. We need to declare, "God, she will come out stronger than when she went in. You, God, are able to do exceeding and abundantly!" But, those words become empty when you have no relationship or experience with His greatness. Your worship becomes a form of flattery to God, and it doesn't garner a response from Him.

Therefore we pray and people stay sick. We pray, and people become worse in the hospital. We pray for money and stay broke. We pray for a different outcome, and it gets worse than we thought it would ever be. Why? Because we don't make prayer an expression of the acts of God and acts of the greatness of God; it must be an expression of who He is. He is great, and He is God of all; that's when your prayer becomes worship.

Jesus is our example of this in Luke 6:12 and He told us in Luke 18:1 to do the same. I don't know how we're going to get around true worship when He did it and He told us to do it. We can't just come in and bellyache, whine, and make excuses and allow our circumstances to tell us what and who God is. We must let our God dictate what the circumstances and the outcome of the circumstances will be. Proseuchomai is the expression and the *act of worship*. When I desire to express and have the act of worship, it's proseuchomai.

He could have used any kind of language: men ought always to praise or men ought always to give thanks. But He said, "Men ought always to pray—proseuchomai—men ought always to *worship*," and in Luke 6:12 it says that He did it all night and commanded us to do likewise.

TALKING POINT

How will this information about worship change your attitude towards worship?

_____

_____

_____

_____

_____

_____

_____

_____

_____

_____

_____

_____

_____

_____

_____

_____

_____

_____

_____

_____

_____

_____

CHAPTER 2

It's an Attitude, a Common Heart

THIS NEXT WORD IS GOING TO BE akin to the word *proseuchomai*, it is *proskynētēs*—the attitude and intent of worship. After we get into the *act* of worship, we must get to the acceptable *attitude*. It's one thing to lift our hands, it's another thing to lift them with the right attitude. It's one thing to say God is great, it's another thing to have the attitude that supports that nothing is bigger than our God!

I was speaking to a young man who said, "I have to go to the school where I am because my father's military benefits don't transfer. His benefits won't transfer to where I want to be." I stopped him in his tracks and said, "God is not a God who's limited by barriers. God can annihilate the barriers. He can get around them like they don't even exist." The young man began to cry and said, "I never thought about it like that. I thought if it was a barrier to me, it was a barrier to God." Every barrier to you is not a barrier to God; every limitation to you is not a limitation to God!

Sometimes, when we think about what we're facing with our children, it looks like it's an impossibility. It looks like they're digging a hole for themselves. It's as if they go and find the worst people they can for friends. Often, it seems as if they go on a hunt to find the most unqualified companion they can to present to their parents. When we look at it, we think, "Where did we go wrong?"

It doesn't say the Father is seeking apostles. It doesn't say He's seeking deacons. He's seeking true worshipers.

All I can tell you is, "Keep worshipping." It is our worship that announces to the heavens that we're trusting God to change the circumstances. We're not letting the limitations dictate the size of our God. We're letting the size of our God handle the limitations and the barriers! Whatever the barrier is, God is able, and He will do it because we're expecting and worshipping, and we know we can't do it and He will have to.

Do you want the attitude of a worshiper or do you just want the act of worship? Where are the true worshipers? First, I discussed the act or expression of worship, and now we will discuss the *attitude* of worship. We have lots of people who attest to the acts of God but lack an attitude of worship.

> "But the hour cometh, and now is, when the true worshipers shall worship the Father in spirit and in truth: for the Father seeketh such to worship him" (John 4:23).

I'm going to follow Jesus and become a *person of worship*, that's *proskynētēs*. The Father is looking for true worshipers; He's looking for the person of worship. It says God seeks such to worship Him. I believe we should want to become true worshipers. It doesn't say the Father is seeking apostles. It doesn't say He's seeking deacons. He's seeking true worshipers. I want to be the person God seeketh!

There is no part of our life that we should feel is off limits to the strength, sovereignty, and power of our God.

We must want our daily lives to demonstrate the strength, the power, and the awesomeness of God in all we say and in all we do. We must set that as the goal and not settle for, "We're just not there yet." We're not going to get there unless we know getting there is a possibility. Too often, the saints use the excuse that God is still working on me. That's a given. God is going to be working on us until we die. We are worshipers! We need to start saying, "I am a worshiper. And in everything that

I do, I'm a worshiper. I don't see any problem too hard because I am a worshiper."

I was in my garage trying to start my power washer for the first time in the season. But it wouldn't start. Finally, I said, "Holy Spirit, cause this thing to start now." I said, "God, You're the God of everything!" And the next pull, it started. I really believe that as a worshiper every part of our life demonstrates the greatness of God. There is no part of our life that we should feel is off limits to the strength, sovereignty, and power of our God. So, when we're facing something, we say, "God, You are God!" We don't let sickness overtake us, we are worshipers! When you're facing sickness, say, "I'm a worshiper." Since the Father is seeking the true worshiper, be that one that He seeks. Have the attitude of a worshiper. It doesn't say He's seeking for anything else other than true worshipers.

Since the Father is seeking the true worshiper, be that one that He seeks.

I want to make myself necessary to God! Jesus did it! I'm becoming a worshiper because He was a Worshiper. If Jesus was a Worshiper and He was God and the Holy Ghost is God, and the Holy Ghost lives in me and He's as much God as Jesus was and they were Worshipers, then I can be a worshiper too! I can state boldly that I'm a worshiper because there's a Worshiper in me! Who's the Worshiper? The Holy Ghost is the worshiper. He reveals who Jesus is, and He honors the Father. If the Worshiper is in me, then I'm a worshiper, and so are you!

Worship can become our nature! As we become worshipers, we lose sight of the limitations in various things that could cause us not to succeed. God is going to figure it out. If it looks like we're not going to have enough money, He's going to get us out of it; we're going to worship Him.

We can complain, or we can worship, but we can't do both.

It's a choice: We can complain, or we can worship, but we can't do both. Either we're going to worry or we're going to worship. I'm not going to see the glass as half-empty. I'm not going to see the problem as though it may not work. I'm a worshiper, and so are you.

As I become a worshiper, I lose sight of barriers and hindrances. I lose sight of anything that could cause hindrances to my excelling or succeeding. The worshiper that's inside of me states boldly that I am able; he states boldly that I will come through this. As a result, success! I'm not going to see the problem as impossible. I'm going to see it as a possibility—God's possibility. It can work if He wants it to work and He is able to make it work. I'm going to see it as if I can do all things. I'm going to see it as if there's nothing that can stop me. I can't fail, I can't falter, I can't lose. I'm going to start looking at my life through the worshiper that I am becoming. That's what I want to encourage you to do: Look at your life through the worshiper that you are becoming. *There is a worshiper in you!*

There are two Greek words from the base of *proseuchomai: proskynētēs*—the act and the attitude of worship, and *proseuchē*—which is to have the commitment of worship.

> "And Jesus said unto them, Because of your unbelief: for verily I say unto you, If ye have faith as a grain of mustard seed, ye shall say unto this mountain, Remove hence to yonder place; and it shall remove; and nothing shall be impossible unto you. Howbeit this kind goeth not out but by prayer and fasting" (Matthew 17: 20-21).

This kind. What is this kind? This kind can only go out by prayer and fasting. This is *proseuchē*: worship and fasting. The same Scripture is found in Mark 9:29, where we see that worship will always address any need. Jesus said, "You have a need here, a need for faith that will address demons." Worship is going to always address needs. If I can become a person of worship, I'm always ahead of my needs.

Look at your life through the worshiper that you are becoming. *There is a worshiper in you!*

"Then came the disciples to Jesus apart, and said, 'Why could not we cast him out?'" (v. 19) Jesus told them: This level of faith comes from a lifestyle of worship! This is a lifestyle. You guys are trying to become super spiritual warriors because of the event. But this that I did is the result of a lifestyle of fasting and praying and worshiping. This kind only comes out because you have a lifestyle of praying and worshiping. This is a commitment!

Worship invokes the presence of God that addresses your need.

Because I live this way, I don't even worry about needs because my worship is addressing needs before I even know they're needs. My lifestyle says: My God is bigger than this need! *Proseuchē* deals with commitment. We don't look at things as though they are greater than God.

If we say things like, "Well God, this is fourth stage cancer. Even though she's thirteen, she's had a good life."

Absolutely not!

Or we say, "It's in the Lord's hands now."

Instead, say, "Absolutely not! God, this child hasn't even begun to live. So, we worship you. We thank you that You can extract the pneumonia from her lungs. Father, we thank you that You can cause the cancer to go into remission. We thank you, God, this isn't the end of this baby's life because You're bigger than this."

Our worship positions us to know that God is always greater than our need. Worship invokes the presence of God that addresses your need. It has to be something you can do no matter what place you find yourself in. My commitment is: No need is greater than God; no place is greater than God. He wants every place where we are to become a place of worship. He wants no place of business to be greater than God. No matter what the situation is, no matter where we are, we can say: "My God can supply my need!" No matter where we are! David said, "If I make my place in hell, you are there." Every place I am is a place of worship.

I was at a funeral that just seemed so sad. When I got to the platform, I said, "Hallelujah!" Because every time the saints get together, it's a hallelujah moment. Even though I'm saying goodbye to a loved one, it's a place of worship. The true worshiper has the nature and commitment to worship.

THE THIEF

> "And said unto them, It is written, My house shall be called the house of prayer; but ye have made it a den of thieves" (Matthew 21:13).

That word in "house of prayer" is *proseuchē*. When we're in a state of mind—in a place—and we don't recognize His greatness, we have made it a den of thieves.

Who is the thief?

> "The thief cometh not, but for to steal, and to kill, and to destroy" (John 10:10).

When we don't recognize His greatness, we have made where we are a den of thieves. We have just given the thief the go-ahead; we've given the thief the green light—we've forgotten who we're dealing with. We've forgotten *proseuchomai*: we should always have an expression of worship (an act of worship), even if it takes all night.

We have forgotten *proskynētēs*: we're worshipers.

We've forgotten *proseuche*: in every place, we are committed to worship.

If you don't make it a place of worship, you have, "made My house of worship a den of thieves."

When we don't recognize His greatness, we have made where we are a den of thieves.

So, if we are in third stage cancer and not acknowledging the greatness of God, we have just opened our situation to the thief. When we don't have any money and we say, "I'll have to get a second job," instead of saying, "My God is able," we've just made our situation open to the thief.

Someone told me I would have to move to New York or LA to fulfill God's vision. I said, "No, I don't agree. God is the God of everywhere. I can live like a New Yorker even in Quincy because I make every place that I am a place of worship!"

"But the hour cometh, and now is, when the true worshipers shall worship the Father in spirit and in truth: for the Father seeketh such to worship him" (John 4:23).

I am a place of worship. There's no place I live that I'm going to let become a den of thieves.

This word *proseuchē* in "house of prayer" is also inter-changeable with "worship" in Mark 11:17 and in Luke 19:46. All of these are the same. Whatever place I am in, it is a place of worship. If the doctor walks in and says you have a tumor on your brain, lift your hands and say, "God is the God of life and health, and He's able to extract the tumor." If I get a notice that my taxes are beyond past due, I say, "God you're the God of all things." I'm not going to get frustrated or panic. I'm going to call on Jehovah. The place where I am has to give God room to get in, so the thief has no auspices, no authority in any situation I'm facing.

Whatever place I am in, it is a place of worship.

"Jesus answered and said unto them, Verily I say unto you, If ye have faith, and doubt not, ye shall not only do this which is done to the fig tree, but also if ye shall say unto this mountain, Be thou removed, and be thou cast into the sea; it shall be done. And all things, whatsoever ye shall ask in prayer, believing, ye shall receive" (Matthew 21:21-22).

All things you ask in *proseuchē*—committed to worship—you can receive! When my attitude and my intent are right, then my request will be right because I will ask without any wavering. I will ask for the mountain to be removed, I will ask for the tumor to be dissolved.

I spoke to the mountain when I said there will be no snow, and the snow went to Wisconsin, New York, and Pennsylvania. In all things, whatsoever we ask in *pro-seuchē*—committed to worship—we ask with nothing wavering, the mountain will be removed. Look at what the Lord is saying: If we ask anything in worship, if we make our request committed in worship, we'll have what we ask.

Don't pray weak prayers to a strong God.

Don't pray weak prayers to a strong God. Don't pray flesh prayers to a spiritual God, a powerhouse God. Make your request known unto God and don't back up. I'm praying for millions for our new development. I prayed, "Father, thank you for the millions of dollars that will come into our hands" and He will do it!

TALKING POINTS

What part of you do you think is attractive to God?

_____

_____

_____

_____

_____

_____

_____

_____

_____

_____

_____

_____

_____

_____

_____

_____

_____

_____

_____

_____

_____

_____

_____

_____

CHAPTER 3

The Posture of Worship

THE NEXT WORD OF WORSHIP reveals the right position, *proskyneō*—to be prostrate, to actually fall upon your knees. When we worship—*proskyneō*—it is actually falling on our knees and touching the ground with our forehead. Who do we know that actually prays like that? The Muslims do, and they're worshipping the wrong god!

"... saying, 'Where is He that is born King of the Jews? for we have seen his star in the east, and are come to worship him'" (Matthew 2:2).

The word picture of *proskyneō* is what a dog does to his master's hand when the owner gets home. The dog licks his hands and his face. *Proskyneō—be prostrate, an expression of respect to a being of superior rank.*

When it's time to worship, there's nothing wrong with you being on your face. There's nothing wrong with you being flat on the ground. There's nothing wrong with you knowing the greatness and the superiority of this God that we are worshipping. It's amazing to me that we want to worship but we won't get on our face. We want to worship, yet we won't fall down. We want to worship, and we won't bend over. We want to worship, and we won't weep. I'm explaining the *right posture for worship*.

Worship is powerful when it is done by a true worshiper.

These words in Greek use prayer and worship interchangeably, showing us the *act*, the *attitude*, and now the *posture* of worship.

LEADING THE WAY

Leaders, we may not always be the worship leader, but we must always be the lead worshipers. Worship is powerful when it is done by a true worshiper. The praise and worship leader must be a worshiper. They project who they are onto the audience. *Worship is caught not taught!*

Praise is not worship and worship is not praise. Praise is thanksgiving for what God has done. Praise deals with the acts of God, not necessarily the person. When we say, "This is the day that the Lord has made," we're talking about what He has done. What is our response?

We will rejoice, praise, and be glad in it. Praise can be done corporately. It should bring the corporate house into oneness. We all come in from different walks of life, different challenges throughout the day, different places economically, maritally, and financially. Praise brings a synchronicity, it brings us together around the acts of God. We can all agree: What a mighty God we serve! We bring *everybody in and around the acts of God.*

Praise is a means to an end. It is not an end in and of itself. It's getting us ready to move further. I think the reason why we don't come into worship is because we don't have the right attitude about the person of God! We don't focus enough on what He's already done.

While worship is an end, it's still a means to another end. Worship is getting you ready for the entrance of the Word of God.

When I come into the service, I begin to praise based on all He's done for me. Then I move from His acts to His person. Then I'm ready to do all that I've talked about—I'm ready to make an expression of worship. Anybody coming into the house, no matter what level they are on spiritually, ought to be able to enter into praise. They should be able to agree that He's a mighty God. You don't have to be deep for that. They ought to be able to agree: "He made a way." They ought to be able to agree: "He saved my soul." They ought to be able to agree on the acts of God.

From there we get into the ways of God and our worship is individualized. That's where we start to split off. We enter into worship individually. We enter into a place, whether the house is or isn't in that place. At this point, it's you and the person of God. Yes, it's you and God. You begin to be intimate with Him, and you meditate on all that He is to you, declaring, "Oh God, You are wonderful." As you move from praise, the acts of God and what He did, you come into worship. You talk about the person of God—who God is.

> ## If the worship doesn't till the ground of your heart, the Word hits up against the flesh.

While worship is an end, it's still a means to another end. Worship is getting you ready for the entrance of the Word of God. The Bible says, "The entrance of thy words giveth light" (Psalm 119:130). Worship tills the ground of your heart. It should neutralize and crucify the flesh so that your heart is open for the Word of God to come in and illuminate your life.

It's amazing that during praise and worship, people sleep in the service. It's because we have sung, but not worshipped. We have not become open enough for our flesh to be destroyed, for it to be neutralized so that we're wide open for the Word to come in. If the worship doesn't till the ground of your heart, the Word hits up against the flesh. If we're not careful, we can begin to contest the Word, because our heart is not open for it to bring in light; the illumination of the Word in our lives.

"In him was life; and the life was the light of men" (John 1:4).

The Word was the life and it was the light of men, so I need that Word more than anything! That's why praise is important, and worship is important. They get us ready for the *Word!* Without the Word, we're not prepared to go out as ambassadors for God. We come and hear a good message, but by the time we get to the car, we've forgotten what was said. Why? Because we were never open enough for the Word to have entrance into our lives.

Praise is thanksgiving for what He's done—the acts of God! When praise is done corporately, it brings us to a place of unity in the house; synchronicity, where we're all together. But when we move into worship, we engage with the person of God out of our personal relationship with Him. And as we worship, our flesh is broken down, our heart is made fallow, and the ground of our heart is tilled up. Now we're not sitting in the house contesting the Word, questioning, nor evaluating. We're letting the Word do what it's supposed to do. The Word is quick and sharp, and as powerful as a two-edged sword, dividing asunder the soul and spirit, joint and marrow (see Hebrews 4:12). The Word is trying to get in there and do a work!

HEART-READY WORSHIP

"Delight thyself also in the Lord: and He shall give thee the desires of thine heart. Commit thy way unto the Lord; trust also in him and He shall bring it to pass ... Cease from anger, and forsake wrath: fret not thyself in any wise to do evil" (Psalm 37:4-5,8).

Let's see what has to happen. We begin to delight ourselves also in the Lord, so He can give us the desires of our heart. The Word "delight" is the Hebrew word which means to become soft, pliable, and moldable. That's what worship has to do. It has to get us to the place where we're pliable, where we're open, and our faith level has come up.

> **When we're praising God with lethargic language, we're *saying* He's mighty but we're not *acting* like He's mighty.**

Don't stay away from worship. It's going to be the announcement of the greatness of God. It's really going to break down the walls and get your flesh to a neutral place so the entrance of the Word will give you the light that you need. I don't want to miss it. What if the worship service doesn't do that? It doesn't matter, we worship wherever we are. That's why the psalmist says to enter His gates with thanksgiving and to come into His courts with praise. When I come in, I already have a right attitude about God.

When we're praising God with lethargic language, we're *saying* He's mighty but we're not *acting* like He's mighty. Worship breaks up our fallow ground and gets us to a place where we are in the right posture and attitude. I love to worship God, to get on my face before Him because I know He's a superior being, and He deserves all that and more!

So, we delight ourselves in the Lord, then He gives us the desires of our heart. A better rendering is that He gives our heart what it ought to desire. We become so pliable, we wouldn't dare interrupt this moment with God by starting to beg for something. When we get into that level of worship, God tells us what He's going to give us; where we're going to go. We're in a place where our heart says, "God, You supply all my needs; I don't have any needs. I don't have any problems." We start knowing that our heart desires what He would have it desire, and we don't dare shift into begging God in that moment, because we're declaring His greatness.

Why would we beg of Him who has already provided for us?

Why would we beg of Him who has already provided for us? Psalm 37:4 is showing us that if we delight—if we become soft, and pliable in His hand—He will cause our heart to know what to desire. Verse 5 states that we're to commit our ways to Him, and the Hebrew meaning for "ways" is your "journey, means or course of life." Commit your manners, habits, and conversation to the Lord, trusting also in Him. Now He's now able to bring it all to pass. Committing means we're resting in the Lord: to be still, to be quiet, to hold our peace, to be astonished.

Worship is much more than we realize. It's breaking down the partitions of our flesh, getting us ready for the entrance of the Word of God. It's getting us ready, so we have no contention and combativeness to the Word of God. Our ways are yielded, we're resting in Him. We cease from anger, we're not worried. The Psalmist says says, "fret not yourself to do evil." You're not worried about anything because, in that level of worship, everything that would have made you worry is broken down. Worship is getting us ready so that the Word can come in, and the entrance of God's Word giveth light.

"In the beginning was the Word, and the Word was with God, and the Word was God. The same was in the beginning with God. All things were made by him; and without him was not any thing made that was made. In him was life; and the life was the light of men. And the light shineth in darkness; and the darkness comprehended it not" (John 1:1-5).

"Comprehend" means the darkness can't stop the penetration of the light—it can't forbid the light. Worship is making the way for us to get the most advantage possible out of the Word of God. We can't jeopardize that. We have to maintain our expression, maintain our commitment to worship, maintain the right attitude and the right posture because that's what gets us ready for the Word. The Word coming in brings so much of His life and light that there's nothing in us that can doubt; no unbelief, no sickness, no darkness can be greater than that light that's coming on the inside of us.

"The entrance of thy words giveth light; it giveth understanding unto the simple" (Psalm 119:130).

His Word is going to give us light, and it's going to give understanding to the simple. If worship doesn't get us ready, we're going to contend, contest, and be combative, and the Word of God will be made of no effect by our tradition and our carnality. Therefore, we're unable to go into the world and be a demonstration of who God is to the world—all because the Word did not get into good fertile soil, because the worship did not get in there and break up the fallow ground. Therefore, the flesh could not receive the Word of God.

Worship is making the way for us to get the most advantage possible out of the Word of God.

Praise is a means to an end, and worship is an end and a means to another end. Praise brings us to worship. Worship breaks up the condition of our heart, neutralizes and weakens the flesh so that the Word can have entrance into us, find itself in good soil and produce fruit a hundred-fold. That's the goal: that praise gets us to worship and worship gets us ready for the Word. Because our hearts have been made fallow through worship, now the Word can have entrance without rocks and stony ground, without distractions, and it can produce great fruit through our lives.

TALKING POINTS

What changes must you make to be a lead worshiper?

_____

_____

_____

_____

_____

_____

_____

_____

_____

_____

_____

_____

_____

_____

_____

_____

_____

_____

_____

_____

_____

_____

_____

_____

_____

CHAPTER 4

Vertical Worship

THERE ARE TWO TYPES OF WORSHIP: vertical worship and horizontal worship. I really believe with all my heart that when the Father seeks for true worshipers, He is talking about those who are focused vertically. Vertical worship is worship that is focused on Him and not on anything that's in the horizontal—in the plain sight of natural vision. The Father is looking for those who will focus their hearts on Him, without distraction, without concern for what's going on in this realm. Remember, Paul said to seek those things which are above where Christ is seated at the right hand of God (see Colossians 3:1).

Once we are vertically focused, we lose sight of ourselves and our circumstances. We forget about who we think we are or who we think we are not. All real true worship is vertical, never horizontal. I don't believe we can worship with our minds on ourselves, on our circumstances or on those who are watching or concerned with who we are or who we are not. Whether we're thinking, "I'm an apostle," or "I'm too unworthy," all of that is horizontal—we want to lose sight of that and focus on *who He is*.

When we focus on who He is, it really doesn't matter who we thought we were or who we thought we were not—we are just lost in the presence of who He is. The more we think about it, we realize that most of our worship has been horizontal. If it talks about things in this realm, such as "praising until we can't see our problems"—it's still horizontal.

When I get so lost in Him that I'm not really thinking about those earthly things, then that gives Him room to deal with them.

What I'm suggesting is a vertical shift. When we worship vertically, we lose sight of everything that's in our view or in this sphere—everything in the realm of Earth. I'm not saying we don't need more money or we don't have the reality of the x-ray or we don't deal with the reality of the numbers or the deadline tomorrow. I'm saying that vertical worship causes us to lose sight of those things.

When I get so lost in Him that I'm not really thinking about those earthly things, then that gives Him room to deal with them because He would rather deal with those things than lose our vertical worship. He wants us to worship because "the Father seeketh such to worship

Him." He's looking for true worshipers, so I want us to begin to focus vertically rather than horizontally.

Then we realize that God is more interested in our attitude about Him than our title or our position in the earthly realm. When we begin to worship Him, His mighty presence brings a relevance *to* us and a relevance *through* us. As we worship vertically, we lose sight of everything else and His presence becomes real. That's why I don't worry about my circumstances. I don't consider that I'm a bishop and I shouldn't do such a thing or that. We can't think about our sin last week or the wrong we did yesterday; we lose sight of all of that because His presence to us and through us is greater than the deficiencies or superiority the enemy wants us to focus on when our flesh desires us to think more highly (or more lowly) of ourselves than we ought.

Vertical worship is what the Father is addressing, He's looking for those that are true (vertical) worshipers.

"But the hour cometh, and now is, when the true worshipers shall worship the Father in spirit and in truth."

The Father looks for the true, vertical worshiper. So I want you to recognize that as you stay focused vertically, things happen."

THE SECRET PLACE

"He that dwelleth in the secret place of the most High shall abide under the shadow of the Almighty. There shall no evil befall thee, neither shall any plague come nigh thy dwelling. He shall call upon me, and I will answer him: I will be with him in trouble; I will deliver him, and honour him" (Psalm 91:1, 10, 15).

In Psalm 91, it's vertical worship that's going to get us into the secret place. On our own, we're not going to be able to get there. If we are focused on or concerned about the position or trouble we're in, our financial disarray or some news about our child, it vies for our attention and prevents us from staying focused on God, from staying in vertical worship and staying in the secret place.

When we don't remain in vertical worship, we disqualify ourselves from the secret place, which is where we want to be. The secret place can be found anywhere because it's about our attitude toward God. For example, Paul and Silas were in jail and because their attitude was right toward God, they could enter the secret place, in that place.

The secret place is not a secret *from* us, it holds the secret *for* us.

A former member of our church was in ICU, and I was called to the hospital. There were five or six doctors in her room. The doctor said, "We're losing her," and wouldn't let me in. So, I made the corridor "the secret place." Where I am, as the vertical worship touches and pierces Heaven, it unlocks the presence of God to come to me and through me to reach the person I'm praying for. I saw her in the line at the bank recently and spoke to her, this woman who was at the point of death. My vertical worship released God to be present in her situation. What if I had said, "They won't let me in so I guess it's over, it's curtains for her. This is horrible. They coded her"? Even though I wasn't in the room where the doctors were, I know God touched her because that woman is alive today three years later.

The secret place is not a secret *from* us, it holds the secret *for* us. It's there for us, and the secrets are in the secret place. As we enter into vertical worship, we unlock the secret place. What is the secret place? It is where the Father reveals Himself to us. In addition to our touching Him, He is touching and communing with us. I always thought, *Who can find the secret place?* They made it sound like a secret, rather than explaining that worshipers can always unlock the secret place because it's not hidden *from* us, it's hidden *for* us. Why? Because we are the true worshipers and the true worshipers have access.

When I unlock the secret place from any place, I have tapped into a realm where God is.

In Psalm 91:1, David gives the revelation of the Psalm. Look at verse one: "He that dwells". This tells us that the Almighty dwells in the secret place. Now if the Almighty is in the secret place, when I unlock the secret place from any place, I have tapped into a realm where God is. We know that God is omnipotent, omniscient, and omnipresent. Therefore, when I begin to worship vertically, I unlock the place where He is abiding. That's letting me know that God will not hide Himself from me in the secret place. His secret place is hidden for me, not from me.

Then I tell the Lord that He is my refuge and my fortress, in Him will I trust, He shall cover me, and so on. That's letting me know He is there. How is He covering if He's not there? Under His wings, I am trusting. His truth is going to be my shield and my buckler, and I don't have to be afraid of the terror by night. That's reminding me I don't have to be fearful or in terror; I can access the secret place from any place, whether day, night, darkness, light, trouble, lots of money, no money, circumstances, situations, pressure, no pressure, or ten thousand at my right hand—none can come near me.

Either we focus on God or focus on our problems.

We have to make a decision to leave the baggage outside the door. We can't worship focusing on our baggage, on our problem, on what we have to deal with. Either we focus on God or focus on our problems. Why go into the secret place where truth can be revealed to us and still worry about what the enemy is saying to us?

Regardless of the situation, it's time to find the secret! God will handle the problems, and He handles them in the secret place. We have to decide: We are not going to shift out of the position of vertical worship. The moment we go horizontal, we have closed the door and left the secret place; then we are forced to deal with our circumstances with our own natural ability. If we stay in vertical worship, we're going to stay in the secret place. The moment we go horizontal, we're going to have to deal with things in the natural. God is looking for such to worship Him—true vertical worshipers—so He can reveal the truth that will defend us. His truth will enlighten us, and it will not forsake us. Only with our eyes will we see trouble.

The instant we worry, we exit the secret place, and we cut off our ability to hear from the secret place.

We can't leave the secret place and worry about our problems. The instant we worry, we exit the secret place, and we cut off our ability to hear from the secret place. We can't hear His secrets and His strategies; we cut off His ability to enlighten us and to deliver us from our situation. Verse 10 says no evil is going to befall us, so why would we leave the secret place? Because I am vertical, God says He will deliver me, and He will set me on high because I have known His name. (The Hebrew word for "name" here is *shem*, which is a mark or memorial of individuality; reputation, fame, glory). In verse 15, it says, "He'll call and I'll answer." The secret place holds His secrets for us not from us, and in that place His secrets are ready to be made known to us. God is in the secret place, where He holds His secrets for us:

I. Creativity: He'll tell you what you can say and what you can do—calling those things that be not as though they were (see Romans 4:17). Creative things come alive; powerful things become available to you. He's going to tell you how to speak, what to speak and what not to speak in the secret place; the secret place which is vertical worship. From the secret place, He's going to make secrets known to you. Your creative genius is going to come alive. He's going to tell you what to say, what to do, what not to say, and what not to do. Stay there, calling things that be not as though they already are—announcing things as He's revealing to you the power that's available to you to change your situation.

As you cease to focus on your situation, how horrible it is, then suddenly you'll have an original strategy.

II. Originality: He's going to give you a way of escape that you didn't know existed. Thoughts are going to come, and you'll begin to know things that you hadn't previously considered.

III. Divine Strategy: He gives you a Divine strategy to know what to do in your situation. As you cease to focus on your situation and how horrible it is, then suddenly you'll have an original strategy. You'll know something you never thought of. You'll do something no one has ever done. You'll say something no one has ever said—all because you visited the secret place. Once you focus your worship vertically, you get into a place that was hidden for you and not hidden from you. That's huge! When it comes to worship, our secret place is hidden for us not from us.

Praise gets us to worship, and worship is a means to another end: the secret place. It's a breaking down of our situation and our circumstances. It makes fallow the ground of our heart and, all of a sudden, we possess a strategy in our heart. It gets us on top of the situation. Now we're ready to consider every truth.

Remember, Psalm 91 says His truth shall be your shield and buckler, and the truth is the "matter as God sees it." Now God's strategy is available. God makes known a strategy, and we begin to see that it's not as bad as we thought because God reveals the strategy out of it. As you "delight thyself also in the Lord," you become soft and pliable, moldable, that means His hand and His presence are on you; He's melting you in vertical worship. He tells your heart what you need to desire. He gives you what to ask for. He'll tell you not to worry about anything!

Now you can trust that God has everything that you need in the secret place.

Psalm 37:5 says I'm going to commit my ways unto the Lord and trust also in Him, God is able to bring that to pass. Remember Psalm 91, "Under His wings shall you trust." Now you're ready to consider every truth. Truth is now available. God reveals a strategy out of it and around it. Now you can trust that God has everything that you need in this place. And it can be found from any place.

Why would you move out of the secret place? You've got to trust that in the secret place you're going to hear truth and find your strategy. *Here* you're going to know what to do; *here* He's going to shield you from the noisome pestilence by day and the arrow that flies by night; *here* he's going to protect you though a thousand fall at your side. You're not going to be moved by any of that. Because you've set your love upon Him and you trust Him, you're not going to exit the secret place until you know what to do because the secret is in there for you.

You have to make a decision: either to worry or to worship—you can't do both.

You cannot worry, you cannot shift from vertical to horizontal, you cannot go back and start worrying. You can't do both. You have to make a decision: either to worry or to worship—you can't do both. The moment you go back to worrying, you shift from vertical to horizontal. Worrying is not accomplishing anything so don't leave the secret place, where His presence is, and where you can get the truth, the creativity, originality and Divine strategy to deal with any and every situation.

You cannot worship and worry! The moment you start to worry, you cease to worship—the moment you start to worship, you cease to worry. If you worship, you will not worry. If you worry, you will not worship. If you worship vertically, you'll get strategies, creativity, and originality because that's where it comes from—the secret place.

You have to get in the secret place and stay there. You have to decide you're not going to move: circumstances are just trying to bring you out of the secret place. There is a way out of worry: it's true worship in the secret place. You have to make a decision that worry hasn't helped you up to now, and that having your thoughts scattered is a temptation. One moment in the secret place can devise a strategy that will serve you for the next year or years. When you lift up worship that is focused on God, in an instant, He can take you to that secret place and give you a strategy. How long you stay there isn't as important as the secrets you get there. It's up to you to find that place from any place.

How long you stay in the secret place isn't as important as the secrets you get there.

We have put it on others to get us into the secret place, but in reality, the moment that our feet hit the ground, we can take 10 seconds, think about how great He is, and be in the secret place.

Worship is an attitude. It's not songs or music; it's a trust in Him to keep us all day. It's acknowledging His greatness. We enter the secret place without song or music, just a proper attitude. It's not that we forget what's on us, it's just that we no longer focus on it. We leave the luggage outside. We know it's there, but we don't take it into the secret place with us. We get the strategy and come out with truth. The secret place helps us to have insight—we do see the luggage, but we will know what to do about it when we come out.

Worship is a natural expression of those with a genuine relationship with God. We can win the world with this teaching. The Holy Spirit of Heaven is the only element that keeps us in touch with Heaven's times table. The world will see a level of peace in us, they will see a level of calmness in us, and the world will want what we have. You cannot worry and worship, and you cannot worship and worry. I don't believe you can teach worship, but you can demonstrate it. Worship is caught not taught because I can't teach you relationship with God; I can demonstrate it, so you can catch it.

Worship is a natural expression of those with a genuine relationship with God.

I'm reminded of one of my teachings: the highest activity in Christianity is *servanthood*, the highest Christian character is *humility* and the highest Christian devotion is *worship*. The proud won't praise: pride won't let you praise and the religious person won't worship. You can't worship while thinking about yourself and what people are going to say.

So we've got to cease trying to improve on what God has already done. Let God be God and get out of pride. Praise is the appropriate vestment, it's the right attire, for the saints of God. We are to be praisers. Praise is a confident boasting in God and we are to be praisers. Praise invites God to come. It's thanksgiving for what He's done, and worship is thanksgiving for who He is. Worship deals with the person of God, and praise deals with the acts of God. Worship is an attitude about God and His ability to be God in every situation.

Praise is thanksgiving for what He's done, and worship is thanksgiving for who He is.

When your relationship is pure and right, the natural thing to do is worship. When you feel like you've just got to sing a song, that is a reflection of the quality of your relationship with God. Someone can have a relationship with the church, they have a relationship with religion, they have a relationship with their title, they have a relationship with their position—but the purity and the genuineness of their relationship with God does not exist, it's lacking.

When it's there, you don't have to encourage them, it's their natural response, their natural expression because they have a genuine relationship with God!

TALKING POINTS

When were you last in the secret place?

_____

_____

_____

_____

_____

_____

_____

_____

_____

What alerts you to the shift of your worship to vertical worship?

_____

_____

_____

_____

_____

_____

_____

_____

_____

_____

CHAPTER 5

The Holy Spirit and Worship

WITHOUT THE HOLY SPIRIT, we will be lost in our effort to engage with God in vertical worship. We need the Holy Spirit! The Holy Spirit is important in our worship experience because He's the one that knows the most about Jesus! Who knows Jesus better than the Holy Spirit, and who knows the Father better than Jesus? As we engage in true worship, we need the Holy Spirit to constantly point us to Jesus who knows the Father best.

The Holy Spirit is God, and who better to tell us about God than God Himself? The Holy Spirit is God, the Holy Spirit knows God, and the Holy Spirit knows us. He is able to show us the Son, and the Son is able to point out the Father, and reveal the Father to us. Therefore, we need the Holy Spirit if we're going to enter into true worship that worships the Father in spirit and in truth.

Because Jesus is the Word, He is truth! The Scripture says that "Thy word is truth" and Jesus is that truth that was made flesh and dwelt among us. So, the Holy Spirit points Him out and Jesus points out the Father! I must have the right attitude about God, and I can't do that unless the Son reveals Him to me.

"Sanctify them through thy truth: thy word is truth" (John 17:17).

"And the Word was made flesh, and dwelt among us, (and we beheld his glory, the glory as of the only begotten of the Father,) full of grace and truth" (John 1:14).

WHY IS THE HOLY SPIRIT SO IMPORTANT IN WORSHIP?

"When Jesus came into the coasts of Caesarea Philippi, He asked his disciples, saying, Whom do men say that I the Son of man am? And they said, Some say that thou art John the Baptist: some, Elias; and others, Jeremiah, or one of the prophets. He saith unto them, But whom say ye that I am? And Simon Peter answered and said, Thou art the Christ, the Son of the living God. And Jesus answered and said unto him, Blessed art thou, Simon Barjona: for flesh and blood hath not revealed it unto thee, but my Father which is in heaven" (Matthew 16:13-17).

The church knows little about Jesus and even less about the Holy Spirit! Jesus said, "Who do people say that I am?" Some said John the Baptist, but that couldn't be true. They were saying that Jesus was the reincarnation of John, who had been beheaded. Some said, "You are Elijah" and, again, He would have had to be the reincarnation of Elijah an Old Testament prophet. And some said Jeremiah or one of the other prophets.

But He said to the disciples, "Who do you say I am?" Simon Peter's response was, "You are the Christ, the Son of the Living God." And Jesus said, "Blessed are you Simon (son of) Barjona, for flesh and blood didn't reveal that to you, but My Father said to you who I am." So, if it's going to take the Father to reveal who the Son is, the Son to reveal who the Father is, and the Holy Spirit to tell us who the Son is—we need the Holy Spirit!

Who knows the Godhead better than God Himself?

Because who knows the Godhead better than God Himself? And the agent of God on Earth today is the Holy Spirit. Peter was able to say, "You are the Christ." Jesus then said, "The Father showed you who the Son is." When you know who the Son is, you can know who the Father is. When you know who the Father is, you can know who the Son is. So Holy Spirit, show me who the Son is so He can likewise show me who the Father is.

"Then answered Jesus and said unto them, Verily, verily, I say unto you, The Son can do nothing of himself, but what He seeth the Father do: for what things soever He doeth, these also doeth the Son likewise. For the Father loveth the Son, and sheweth him all things that himself doeth: and He will shew him greater works than these, that ye may marvel. For as the Father raiseth up the dead, and quickeneth them; even so the Son quickeneth whom He will" (John 5:19-21)

Here's the connection between the Father, Son, and Holy Ghost. You need the Holy Ghost to show you the Word of God, the truth that's in the Word, and the Word of God shows you who the Father is. Then you can have the right attitude about the Father and know the truth about the Son. You can read the Bible, the letter of the law, from cover to cover and never discover Jesus. You can read from Genesis to Revelation and never discover Jesus. Who shows you who Jesus is? The Holy Spirit!

You can read the Bible, the letter of the law, from cover to cover and never discover Jesus.

We never knew who the fourth man was in the fiery furnace: Jesus. We never knew that the rod that parted the Red Sea (the Bible said the sea saw Him), was Jesus. All the way through the Bible from Genesis to Revelation, the Holy Spirit points out that that's Jesus. He shows who the Son is—who Jesus is—so that we can properly determine who the Father is and then we can enter into true worship. It's impossible to worship the Father in spirit and in truth without the Holy Spirit. Because the Holy Spirit points out who Jesus is, and Jesus shows us who the Father is, now we can get our attitude right toward God!

Once we pray the Word, we release the strategy and announce the solution! Don't keep speaking about the problem, speak about the solution. Declare the strategy! Let the Holy Spirit unlock the Scriptures. You know what you're going through but don't know how to get out of it. The Holy Spirit is always there, constantly revealing Jesus to us and making Him relevant and available everywhere and anywhere, with strategies and solutions that guarantee victory.

The Holy Spirit is always there, constantly revealing Jesus to us and making Him relevant and available.

The whole purpose of the Holy Spirit is to reveal Jesus to us and make Him relevant and available. If you're in the hospital, make Jesus available there. If you don't have any money, make Jesus available there. Sometimes the Holy Spirit will require you to be a part of the solution.

Without a revelation of Jesus, you're never going to get the correct attitude toward the Father because it's the Word of God that reveals to us who the Father is. Without the Holy Spirit, we don't properly assess the right truth or revelation from the Word of God. We read that He's mighty, but we don't comprehend that He's Mighty. We read that He provides for all our needs, but we don't comprehend that He provides for all our needs. Without a revelation of Jesus, which the Holy Spirit gives us, we don't get the right assessment of Jesus. Thus, we don't have the right attitude toward the Father and we can't really enter into true worship.

STRATEGIES REVEALED

It's the Word of God that gives us the right perspective of the Father. We can't know the Father without the Word of God. From Genesis to Malachi we were told to expect the Word. From Matthew to Acts we saw the Word made flesh, Jesus. But from Acts until now, it takes the Holy Spirit to activate the Word in and through our lives to make Him available to the world.

Jesus is the action part of the Godhead. The Holy Spirit is the revealing part.

I don't want to just read it, I want to live it. I saw Jesus do it, and the works He did He told me I can do—but I need the Holy Spirit so that I can begin doing them. Doing what? Laying hands on the sick so they can recover. Doing what? Raising the dead. Doing what? Seeing miracles everywhere we go. Doing what? Destroying the works of darkness. How are we going to do that? Only if the Holy Spirit is alive and available to us, and we've engaged Him. He's makes Jesus real, He's making the Word of God real and He's making it all relevant to us and through us!

Jesus is the action part of the Godhead. The Holy Spirit is the revealing part—He reveals what actions we ought to take. The Holy Spirit reveals what action is appropriate in every situation. We must clearly see that it is the

Holy Spirit that makes Jesus relevant and real to us. This is what corrects our attitude toward the Father. We can't know the greatness of God, the power of God, who the Father is, without the Word. And we can't know the Word without the Holy Spirit helping to reveal and interpret it for us. The Holy Spirit breaks down the Word for us, and the Word reveals who the Father is.

It is the Holy Spirit that makes Jesus relevant and real to us.

When the Holy Spirit comes upon you, Heaven has endowed you to reveal strategies. You can tell when somebody has been in this secret place because they don't talk normally. They don't talk struggle, they don't talk weak. They speak the strategies that make problems seem small.

> "And, behold, I sent the promise of my Father upon you: but tarry ye in the city of Jerusalem, until ye be endued with power from on high" (Luke 24:49).

This power that's coming upon us is endowing us to give us what we'll need when we come out of the secret place. We come out of the secret place with strategies to function and change our whole world! We have business ideas, we have ways to do things in the marketplace that others don't think about. Why? Because they haven't been in the secret place. We pray for people and they get miracles and people wonder why they didn't see that. Why? They haven't found the secret place. We're endowed with Heaven's secrets and we have a strategy to change the whole atmosphere. The secrets enable us to talk in a way that others don't and to know things that others don't know. The Holy Spirit downloads these strategies and secrets that are held for us in the secret place. We don't stay in the secret place: we get the secrets, we come out and change our world. We function in a way that others do not function!

The Holy Spirit downloads the strategies and secrets that are held for us in the secret place.

Jesus did nothing on Earth as God but as a man.

"The Spirit of the Lord is upon me, because He hath anointed me to preach the gospel to the poor; he hath sent me to heal the brokenhearted, to preach deliverance to the captives and recovering of sight to the blind, to set at liberty them that are bruised, To preach the acceptable year of the Lord" (Luke 4:18-19).

"Jesus saith unto her, Go call thy husband, and come hither. Come see a man, which told me all things that ever I did: is not this the Christ?" (John 4:16, 29)

As Jesus walked being sensitive to the Holy Spirit, He knew all things. By knowing all things, He was able to reveal to the woman at the well, in the above Scripture, the strategy needed to change her world. He said to her, "Go and get your husband." Jesus, walking under the influence of the Holy Spirit, knew that this woman had five husbands. He gave her a strategy to fix her situation. With this strategy, the woman left her water-pot and went away into the city and began to evangelize. Jesus knew what to tell her so that when she applied those strategies and secrets, it changed her life. This woman would probably have been on her eighth or ninth husband if she had not met the Water that would cause her to never thirst in her life again.

That's our job, not going into the secret place and just stay there. Our world needs us to come out and change it. Once we get these secrets and begin to know these things, we need to come out and do something about our world. The Holy Spirit enables us to know all things, past, present, and strategies for the future. God told her about her past and gave her a strategy for the future.

The Holy Spirit enables us to know all things, past, present, and strategies for the future.

The reason many aren't getting a lot done is because they don't know what to do. You can only do what you know, and you know what you know when you see what you do. You always do what you know first. If you don't know anything else to do, you're always left to do what you've always done. But when you know to do different-ly, you do differently! You change your world with the secrets from the secret place.

"And such as do wickedly against the covenant shall he corrupt with flatteries: but the people that do know their God shall be strong and do exploits" (Daniel 11:32).

As I said in Chapter One, worship becomes flattery when we say things about God we don't mean. That's why when people tell me, "Let's give Him a hand of praise," I say, "What's that?" Let me give God my best while I have the best to give. "Those that do know their God." What we know about God, we find in the secret place. What the Holy Spirit reveals to us is what we know. Once we get into the secret place and begin to know Him, we come away with strategies for life.

The Holy Spirit points out things about you and about your past.

I want to emphasize that these secrets and strategies have to do with making you know things present, things past, and strategies about things going forward. That alone should set your life on fire. In your time of worship, you self-correct. The Holy Spirit points out things about you and about your past. When He begins to point them out, it's truth. If He tells you, "You are a liar," trust me, you're a liar. Just repent and go on. He's able to tell you about your present, your past, and your future, giving you strategies so you can go forward and begin to do exploits.

The secrets from the secret place will give you what to do to change your world and those connected to you. These strategies come to you to affect those connected to you and everything that's in their environment.

"But after long abstinence Paul stood forth in the midst of them, and said, Sirs, ye should have hearkened unto me, and not have loosed from Crete, and to have gained this harm and loss. And now I exhort you to be of good cheer: for there shall be no loss of any man's life among you, but of the ship. For there stood by me this night the angel of God, whose I am, and whom I serve, Saying, Fear not, Paul; thou must be brought before Caesar: and, lo, God hath given thee all them that sail with thee. Wherefore, sirs, be of good cheer: for I believe God, that it shall be even as it was told me" (Act 27:21-25).

When you get in the secret place, you start knowing what the enemy's up to. The Holy Spirit exposes the enemy, He exposes the darkness and makes it the same as light to you.

The angel stood by Paul and gave him a strategy, "You've got to get where you're going and I'm going to get you there and everybody connected to you." The strategies are for me and all those connected to me. The secret place gives a strategy to Paul and everyone connected to him. When you get in the secret place, you start knowing what the enemy's up to. The Holy Spirit exposes the enemy, He exposes the darkness and makes it the same as light to you. What if you exposed the lies of your children, exposed your children's actions? They would stop. What if you began talking to your employer and giving them strategies and ideas?

Why does the church seem to be the most unproductive, the last to comprehend new ideas and new ways, when the Holy Spirit can tell us past, present, and future? I think it's time for us to realize He's going to expose the devil. He's going to show us who we are going forward so that our lives and everything connected will bear the fruit of a true worshiper that dwells in the secret place.

TALKING POINTS

Do you engage the Holy Spirit as a person?

_____

_____

_____

_____

_____

_____

_____

_____

_____

_____

_____

_____

_____

_____

_____

_____

_____

_____

_____

_____

_____

_____

_____

CHAPTER 6

Worship and the Gifts of the Spirit

A S YOU ENTER INTO WORSHIP, be aware that you're going to experience the highest level of sensitivity to the gifts of the Spirit that can be acquired. In other words, worship lifts you to a place of sensitivity that enables you to operate in the gifts of the Spirit powerfully.

I don't say: "I'm not a prophet, I don't flow in the gifts, I don't have the gift of healing, I don't have the gift of faith working in me." Once you worship and move into that arena with vertical worship, you are more enabled and more sensitive to the gifting of the Holy Spirit than at any other time. You have been elevated and lifted to a place where the gifts are ready for use.

Scripture says in John 14:2, "In my Father's house there are many mansions," many secret places. There are many—the King James says—"mansions." As you worship, the gifts of the Spirit are at peak ability to operate through you because you've come to a place where you've shed the flesh, you've shed carnality, you've shed you!

We have always thought of the gifts of the Spirit as some super spiritual place. I always hear people say, "I don't operate in that, or I don't operate in those gifts." They're always excusing themselves. But if you enter into worship, it will elevate you to a place of sensitivity. Once you know that sensitivity gets you to the gifts of the Spirit, it's just a matter of using your faith to operate them!

As you worship, the gifts of the Spirit are at peak ability to operate through you.

I'm not a prophet, but many times I see people's futures. I see it and I'm able to walk over to them and announce it: "The Lord told me He is getting ready to do this for you." I'm not a prophet, but through my apostolic gift, I can operate in all of the five-fold offices. But I believe it's *true worship* that heightens my sensitivity to the gifts of the Spirit. There are times I come to the platform with just a blank slate in my spirit. I'm not thinking I want to prophesy to this one or I have a word of knowledge for that one; I'm not thinking that God is going to heal anybody, I'm just glad to be in the presence of the Lord. But as I worship, I have this heightened sensitivity to the gifts of the Spirit.

I don't want you to think this is off limits to you because you're not an apostle, a prophet or another office. I want you to know it's the worship that brings you to that place and ability to flow. All you need is the execution of your faith.

The gifts of the Spirit are available, and you become more sensitive to them than ever before as you worship.

All you need to do is go ahead and say what you have received: "God told me that your legs and your knees are swollen, and you've been struggling." You could have just gotten out of your car from the secret place and walked into Walmart, and you see a person and know that they're struggling with high blood pressure. Are you going to execute your faith and go over to that person because you've got that heightened sensitivity; or are you going to deny what you're feeling and what you're sensing and cheat that person out of an encounter with the Holy Spirit? The gifts of the Spirit are available, and you become more sensitive to them than ever before as you worship.

Let's look at Benny Hinn. People want to make him a teacher and a prophet or a miracle worker or a healing evangelist. Really, in essence, Benny Hinn is a worshiper. As he worships, he's able to be aware of what the Holy Spirit is wanting to do and is currently doing.

He was here, in Quincy, and I was his worshipping organist because he recognized my ability to flow in the gifts as I worshipped, and my ability to be sensitive to the Holy Spirit. So, I have seen him begin to worship and just shift into the operation of the nine gifts of the Spirit.

You don't have to wait until you have an ordination, a coronation or an affirmation or go into the five-fold ministry.

The worshiper can flow in the gifts as one endowed to bring Heaven to Earth. The big challenge is the worshiper's ability to operate in and execute faith.

"Now concerning spiritual gifts, brethren, I would not have you ignorant. Ye know that ye were Gentiles, carried away unto these dumb idols, even as ye were led. Wherefore I give you to understand, that no man speaking by the Spirit of God calleth Jesus accursed: and that no man can say that Jesus is the Lord, but by the Holy Ghost. Now there are diversities of gifts, but the same Spirit. And there are differences of administrations, but the same Lord. And there are diversities of operations, but it is the same God which worketh all in all. But the manifestation of the Spirit is given to every man to profit withal" (1 Cor. 12:1-7).

Verse 1 says, "I don't want you to be ignorant." As you worship, you have access to the gifts! You don't have to wait until you have an ordination, a coronation or an affirmation or go into the five-fold ministry. As you worship, you become aware of what the Holy Spirit is wanting to do and is currently doing.

We know that the Holy Spirit, God the Father, and Jesus are the same. The manifestation of the Spirit is given to every man so they can have advantage in this life. Our challenge is that God reveals, and we don't execute our faith to release those gifts so that people can profit. Verse 7 says, "That every man can profit," every man is advantaged as we worship.

We have all nine gifts of the Spirit available to us via our worship experience.

We're challenged, "Did I really hear God?" What if we call out something and the people aren't here? What if we pray and nothing happens? What if our gifting is rejected? It's not because we're not sensitive to the gift; it's because we didn't let our faith level rise. So we couldn't act, we couldn't release, and we couldn't engage the gifts of the Spirit. We have all nine gifts of the Spirit available to us via our worship experience.

"For to one is given by the Spirit the word of wisdom; to another the word of knowledge by the same Spirit; To another faith by the same Spirit; to another the gifts of healing by the same Spirit; To another the working of miracles; to another prophecy; to another discerning of spirits; to another divers kinds of tongues; to another the interpretation of tongues: But all these worketh that one and the selfsame Spirit, dividing to every man severally as he will" (1 Cor. 12:8-11).

Verse 8 says, "given by the Spirit." Therefore, he that worships, must worship in spirit and in truth. The gifts, and the sensitivity to them, are available to you by your worship. Sometimes as you're counseling people, though they don't know it, you've slipped into vertical worship because God's shared something with you. All of a sudden, you're sensitive to the gifts of the Spirit and you minister to them prophetically.

The challenge is never going to be whether or not the Spirit is moving, but whether you are going to act in faith.

The challenge is never going to be whether or not the Spirit is moving, but whether you are going to act in faith. You're going to start having an awareness because as you elevate in worship, the more sensitive you become. Worship heightens our sensitivity to the Spirit. So be aware that the worship experience, the secret place experience in vertical worship, will unlock strategies, reveal secrets, and make you more aware of the nine gifts of the Spirit. Then, all you need is your faith to kick in to start moving in those gifts.

Now you're operating in the gifts of the Spirit: you'll have words of knowledge and prophecy, you'll speak about healings, and your faith is there. You are now able to operate in any one of the nine gifts of the Spirit!

The worship experience for the worship leader, for the worship teams, and the lead worshiper is not just singing songs, it's not just singing melody, it's not just singing harmony—it's about getting into a place of worship vertically where God can flow through them to start ministering wholeness, health, and healing.

Your worship experience will get you to the place where you can make Jesus known, make Him relevant and make Him available.

We distance ourselves from these gifts by saying things like: "It's not my flow; that's not who I am." Though it may not be your flow, it's worship that's giving it to you. I'm not naturally a minister of healing but worship takes me to that place. I'm not naturally a prophet but worship takes me to that place. One of those nine gifts of the Spirit is faith and all of a sudden, I have a boldness and an ability to believe God and say what God is going to do. As you worship, your faith rises as well.

The world has everything but an authentic Jesus. They have the money, they have the technology, they just don't have an authentic, bona fide, relevant Jesus. Your worship experience will get you to the place where you can make Him known, make Him relevant and make Him available. As with Paul when he was on the ship to Rome, he got a strategy and convinced everyone that was with him to stay on the sinking ship. The people on the ship realized *that man knew God!* That's all we want, for people to be able to access our God. As Daniel prophesied, "They that do know their God will be strong and do exploits" (Dan. 11:32).

But if you don't exercise your faith, you won't act and people won't profit.

TALKING POINTS

What gifts of the Spirit have you been able to operate in when you worship?

_____

_____

_____

_____

_____

_____

_____

_____

_____

_____

How will you execute your faith as you worship?

_____

_____

_____

_____

_____

_____

_____

_____

_____

CHAPTER 7

Pride, an Enemy of Worship

I REALLY BELIEVE THAT AN ATTITUDE of humility is another component that proceeds out of your worship experience: *true* humility. For people that are combative toward God or His Word, worship takes all the fight out of them. When you are a true worshiper, you're trying to find the middle ground; you're trying to find a win-win. You're not coming in with boxing gloves on and guards held high because you know the objective is to minister to people. I believe that as we enter worship, something happens in our hearts that brings us to a place of humility.

"Let this mind be in you, which was also in Christ Jesus: Who, being in the form of God, thought it not robbery to be equal with God: But made himself of no reputation, and took upon him the form of a servant, and was made in the likeness of men: And being found in fashion as a man, he humbled himself, and became obedient unto death, even the death of the cross" (Philippians 2:5-8).

"Let this mind be in you, which was also in Christ Jesus." Instead of, "Let this mind be in you," the Greek renders it, "Have this mind in you." Rather than the idea of "I've got to get it," you have to realize *you already have it*. You just have to yield to it. The Holy Spirit allows you to humble yourself, to reach that win-win situation. The Holy Spirit is a gentleman, He's not trying to start fights. We *have* that mind, we have it! We just need to be aware that we have it and learn how to yield to it through worship.

As you enter into worship, you're going to find yourself losing your desire for a reputation.

"Let this mind be in you (or yield to this mind which is in you), which was also in Christ Jesus: Who, being in the form of God, thought it not robbery to be equal with God." In other words, knowing who I am but carrying myself as if it doesn't matter.

Verse 7 says, "made himself of no reputation," but sometimes we do just the opposite. We make a reputation and try live by it. Jesus had a reputation, but made Himself of no reputation, and said, "Let me find a place to serve." As you enter into worship, you're going to find yourself losing your desire for a reputation. Instead, you'll say, "How can I help you? How can I serve you?" Rather than "let's fight," you'll say: "How can I help you? What can we do to resolve this and really see the Kingdom advance?" Jesus was always in the form of a servant and looking for a place to serve. Verse 8 says, "And being found in fashion as a man, he humbled himself," and that's what you have to do. Obey whatever the Father is dictating, whatever the Holy Spirit is dictating, and leading you to do. The next time you feel like you are to shake somebody's hand in Walmart and you don't, question whether it is a lack of faith, or fear, or pride. If it's fear, what are you afraid of? Rejection, embarrassment, or is it a masking of pride?

God wants our worship to play out in the marketplace, not just in the house.

Jesus was a servant to the world, and so I must become an effective servant bringing in the harvest. I'm an effective worshiper but I'm more in my element in my house. God wants our worship to play out in the marketplace, not just in the house. Therefore, we must pray: "God help us to humble ourselves to do Your will." We must pray: "God help us to move out of this subtle pride," because we don't want our pride to cost other people their victory.

Let's again look at the young Samaritan lady in John 4:7-30. The Samaritans were a mix, a hybrid, transported out of the Babylonian captivity. During that experience, the Jews started mingling with other nations—they weren't in their own element. The Samaritans heralded from the tribe of Manasseh. They became so defiant that they created their own version of the Torah.

The more you worship, the more you are able to come to terms with you.

The reason this young lady had five husbands was because the Jewish law said the maximum number of marriages allowed was three. But the Samaritans had twisted the law, so she had had five husbands. Her interaction with Jesus was wonderful, she brought up the point: "How are you, a Jew, even talking to me? Jews don't speak to Samaritans." You know the Samaritans had some connection with the Jewish lineage because she called Jacob her father. Yet, in verse 29, she's willing to go and confront the men and say, "Come and see a man who knew everything I've ever done." This woman becomes an evangelist, and she realizes her worship has made her into another person. She goes back to those men and says, "I found the Messiah."

With one encounter of worship, her whole life was changed. She must have humbled herself. How else could she have gone to those men who may have been abusive to her? We must humble ourselves, get out in the world, and minister. The truth reveals you to yourself. The more you worship, the more you are able to come to terms with you. You see, we are either full of pride, or we don't want to be rejected. That's why we don't say anything, or we don't witness or we don't minister.

The more we worship, the more we realize who we are, and we can stop fronting. Because we have become a *true worshiper*, the Holy Spirit reveals us to ourselves and reveals Jesus to us so we can represent Him in the Earthly realm. We can't do that as long as we're deceiving ourselves about where we are and who we are. To be a worshiper, we must be in tune with who we are and who we are not.

To be a worshiper, we must be in tune with who we are and who we are not.

The true worshiper becomes a humble person. The truth reveals you to you, and Him to you so that you can make Him available to all those connected to you. Humility gets you out of the way and destroys the pride aspect so that you can become a real instrument, a faithful minister, and a servant of the Most High God.

TALKING POINT

Is your unwillingness to obey, fear or pride?

_____

_____

_____

_____

_____

_____

_____

_____

_____

_____

_____

_____

_____

_____

_____

_____

_____

_____

_____

_____

_____

_____

_____

_____

CHAPTER 8

Worship, a Key to Greater Faith

ROMANS 10:17 SAYS, "So then faith cometh by hearing, and hearing by the word of God." I believe worship is key to a greater faith. And I believe my faith walk is tied to my worship. It's not because I sing. I believe it's because I *worship*—my attitude towards God creates greater levels of faith in me.

I'm proposing that worship is a key to greater faith because of this word "hearing" in the Greek—*akouó*. The etymology of that word in the text takes you back to this: knowing that you are in an audience with God. Faith comes when you know that you have an audience with God, and we can say, "God told me to do that, God revealed that to me." I think that's where we miss it, we're not sure who told us what to do. We're not sure who's going to back the promise we heard. But when I know I've had an audience with God, then faith cometh.

Hearing (Strong's Concordance number 191, *akouó*) means: "give or to get in the audience." When you're in the audience, when it comes to your ears, your hearing is different if you know that God has said it. You'll hear it differently, and you'll act on it differently. When I know that God has said it, I can't be talked out of it even by myself. That's how great faith is born.

When I know that God has said it, I can't be talked out of it even by myself.

I think that when your worship is vertical, it gets you in an audience with God. When you are in an audience with God, then you can serve horizontally. That comes out of knowing that the ultimate audience is the audience of One. Faith is born, and now you can operate horizontally. The gifts of the Spirit can flow and you believe things will happen because God told you He was going to do them. You didn't make it up. Once I know God's said it, I know He's going to back it!

Faith comes when I'm in an audience of One. Out of my vertical audience, I'm able to see and give to my horizontal audience. So, worship creates great faith. Worship is a key to great faith; it's all tied to worship. How are you going to have great faith when you're not a worshiper? When you don't have the right attitude toward God and you've got all your baggage in your prayer closet with you, rather than shutting the door and staying focused and getting that strategy from God?

Someone struggling in their marriage said, "I'm lonely." I said, "Don't confess that, Satan will give you a parade of options." Then he asked what he should do with his feelings, and I told him to pray in the Holy Ghost—prayer in tongues will cancel your negative feelings and emotions. Prayer is worship. We are to always pray and not faint. Get into a vertical place—your secret place!

Prayer in tongues will cancel your negative feelings and emotions.

Surely you don't want to start confessing out of your baggage? You don't want to start saying what you feel. If you don't know what to say, pray in the Holy Ghost. Romans says: When you don't know what to pray, pray in the Holy Ghost! "Likewise the Spirit also helpeth our infirmities; for we know not what we should pray for as we ought" (Romans 8:26).

I hope I have conveyed a perspective of and about worship that will allow you to pray and to worship as you ought. When we don't pray the Word, we won't say the Word, nor communicate a proper attitude about our God. With ease, vertical worship will move you from a place of barrenness to an attitude towards God that opens a whole new world to you!

TALKING POINTS

When were you last in an audience with God?

_____

_____

_____

_____

_____

_____

_____

_____

_____

What sure word proceeded out of His mouth to you?

_____

_____

_____

_____

_____

_____

_____

_____

_____

_____

About the Author

Dr. E.L. Warren is the founder and president of E.L. Warren Ministries International, Inc., a ministry releasing the revelation put in his heart by the Holy Ghost for the equipping of the Body of Christ.

He has been the Senior Pastor of The Cathedral of Worship since December 1980. In 1996, he was Affirmed and set apart to the five-fold office of Apostle to the Body of Christ and was Consecrated to the office of Bishop by the International Communion of Charismatic Churches (ICCC) College of Bishops. Archbishop Earl Paulk presided at the Cathedral of Chapel Hill in Atlanta (Decatur), Georgia in October 1998 and presided at the Installation in Quincy, Illinois in September 1999.

Dr. E.L. Warren has been seen and heard daily on television and radio and travels the world bringing foundation, integrity, and excellence to the Body of Christ in churches, prisons, seminars, conferences, and crusades.

He is the author of seven other books: *Fasting God's Way*; *Positioning Your Faith to Pray the Will of God*;

Healing: A Different Perspective; *I'm Saved, Now What?; Making Your Marriage & Life Marvelous*; *Help Lord, I'm Raising a Teenager* and *The Seduction of Success*. He has written work books for the Institute of Victory, a Ministry School of Excellence, as well as a manual for new convert training. He has also written articles for many magazines and serves as the Senior Advisor for the Sparkman Magazine. He has composed several songs and has recorded and released: "All Things New," "I Trust you Lord," "So Amazing," and over 30 more.

He has served as a board member of G.M.A.C., an outreach of Oral Roberts University; the Administrative Review Board for Illinois Department of Corrections; a former member of Quincy Rotary East, and Advisor for Women's Aglow of Quincy. He is a recipient of the Quincy Jaycee's Top Young Religious Leaders Award in 1983 and has served on Adams County United Way Board, the Adams County Family Services Board, and the Great Commission Radio Board.

Dr. E.L. Warren currently serves as the office of Secretary/Treasurer for the College of Bishops of the (ICCC) International Communion of Charismatic Churches, under the leadership of Archbishop Kirby Clements, also on the Sacred College of Bishops for *Go Tell It Ministries Worldwide,* alongside the leadership of Bishop Corletta Vaughn.

He is the founder of *Goal Setting Systems & Structure Leadership Training.* He has traveled to over 23 Nations and his ministry reaches nearly 10,000 men and women annually in 23 prisons across five states. He is the Chancellor for seven Extension Campuses for Life Christian University. Dr. E.L. Warren is the Presiding Prelate and the COO of the International Network of Affiliate Ministries (INAM).

Dr. E.L. Warren was born to Eddie and Arleather Warren in Baldwyn, MS. He attended and graduated from St. Louis Public Elementary and High Schools. He also attended St. Louis University, St. Louis Christian College, and graduated from Bailey Technical School; and recently received his PhD in Theology from Life Christian University. He served as a Minister of Music at New Northside M.B. Church 1970-1978. E.L. Warren was born again, and Spirit filled in 1976. He accepted his call to ministry in 1978 and was licensed and ordained at New Northside M.B. Church in 1978 by Rev. Willie Ellis. Dr. E.L. Warren has been married since June 1978. His wife is the former Ella Pearl Rockingham. Their children are Valecia Warren, Dr. Malessa Warren, Roderick Warren MBA, and Eddie Cardell Gaston is the oldest son of E.L. Warren. They currently reside in Quincy, Illinois where the Ministry's Corporate Headquarters is established.